FAVORITE
CAT BREEDS

SCOTTISH FOLDS

by Mary Ellen Klukow

AMICUS | AMICUS INK

Amicus High Interest and Amicus Ink are published by Amicus
P.O. Box 1329, Mankato, MN 56002
www.amicuspublishing.us

Copyright © 2020 Amicus. International copyright reserved in all
countries. No part of this book may be reproduced in any form without
written permission from the publisher.

Library of Congress Cataloging-in-Publication Data
Names: Klukow, Mary Ellen, author.
Title: Scottish folds / by Mary Ellen Klukow.
Description: Mankato, Minnesota : Amicus/Amicus Ink, [2020] | Series:
  Favorite cat breeds | Audience: K to Grade 3. | Includes index.
Identifiers: LCCN 2018049612 (print) | LCCN 2018050313 (ebook) | ISBN
  9781681518596 (pdf) | ISBN 9781681518190 (library binding) | ISBN
  9781681525471 (paperback)
Subjects: LCSH: Scottish fold cat—Juvenile literature. | Cat
  breeds—Juvenile literature.
Classification: LCC SF449.S35 (ebook) | LCC SF449.S35 K58 2020 (print) |
  DDC 636.8—dc23
LC record available at https://lccn.loc.gov/2018049612

Photo Credits: iStock/GlobalP cover, 2; Shutterstock/Irina Sokolovskaya
5; Alamy/Sergey Fayzulin 6; Getty/LightFieldStudios 8–9; Getty/Werner
LAYER 10; Getty/Tetsuya Irisawa 12–13; Shutterstock/Moscow Aerlial 14;
Getty/lafar 16–17; Alamy/Natalya Onishchenko 18–19; Shutterstock/
struna 21; Shutterstock/Nejron Photo 22

Editor: Alissa Thielges
Designer: Ciara Beitlich
Photo Researchers: Holly Young and Shane Freed

Printed in the United States of
America

HC 10 9 8 7 6 5 4 3 2 1
PB 10 9 8 7 6 5 4 3 2 1

TABLE OF CONTENTS

SWEET AND LOVING

Look at those floppy ears! That's a Scottish Fold cat. They are known for their sweet personality. Folds are loving and friendly.

ROUND CATS

Scottish Folds are round cats. They have chubby bodies. Their eyes and faces are round. Their tails are **blunt**. Some people think they look like owls.

A NEW LOOK

The first Fold lived in Scotland in 1961. Her name was Susie. Her kittens were **lop-eared**, too. People loved the new look. The cats were bred with British Shorthairs to create the Scottish Fold breed.

Fun Fact
Scottish Folds were first called "lops." Their ears looked like a rabbit's lop-ears.

FOLDED EARS

Scottish Folds have ears that fold forward. This is a **mutation** in their **genes**. Their ears don't stay up. Because of this, some Folds have health problems. They might not hear very well. But they are just as loving as other cats.

SILLY POSES

Scottish Folds can look silly. They are famous for their funny poses. Folds like to stand on their back legs. Some even sit like people!

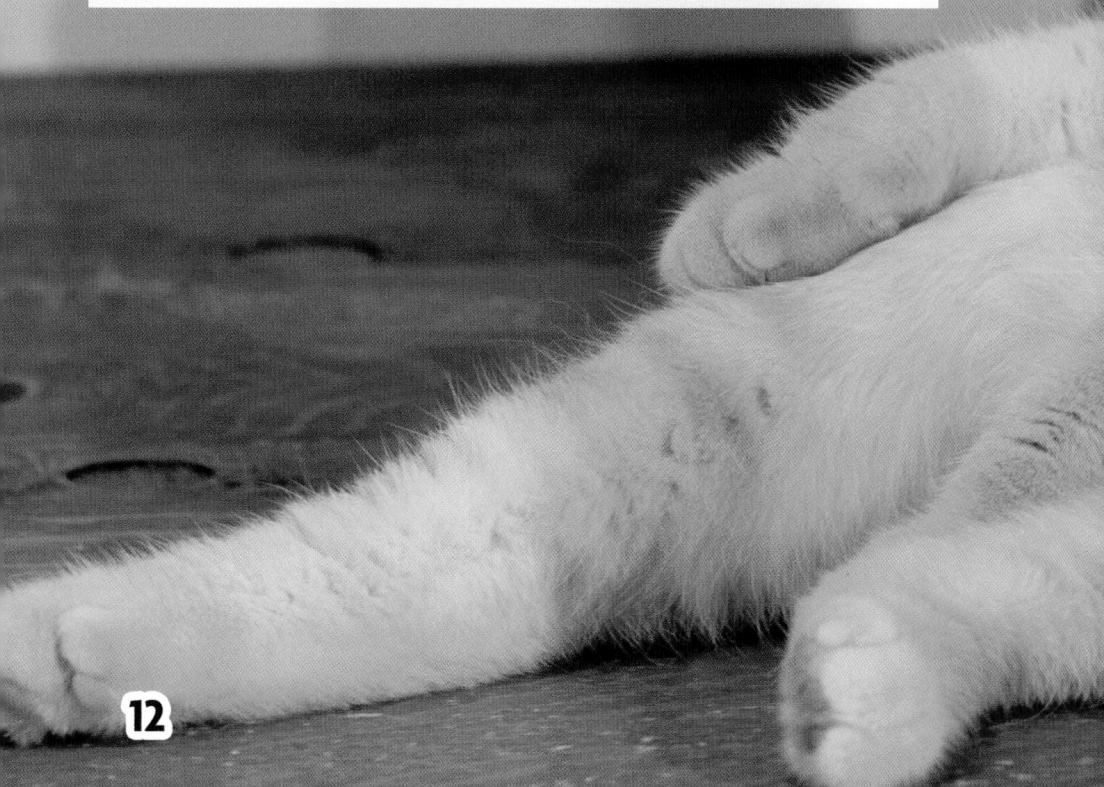

WARM COAT

Folds have **plush** coats. They are warm. Their fur can be long or short. Folds with long fur are sometimes called Highland Folds. Their fur comes in many colors.

Like a Wild Cat?
Siberian tigers have thick, plush coats, too. It keeps them warm in their snowy home.

QUIET CATS

Some cats are loud and talkative. Folds are not. They rarely meow. If they do, it is quiet. They love to purr, though.

Like a Wild Cat?
Bobcats don't make a lot of noise, either. It helps them sneak up on prey.

KITTENS

Two kittens play with each other. They are young Scottish Folds. Their ears are straight now. They will fold when they are three weeks old.

Fun Fact:
Some Scottish Fold kittens' ears never fold at all. They have normal straight ears.

HOUSE CATS

Scottish Folds do best indoors. They are not good at protecting themselves. They are **laid-back** and friendly. Folds love to cuddle and be with their families. They make great pets.

HOW DO YOU KNOW IT'S A SCOTTISH FOLD?

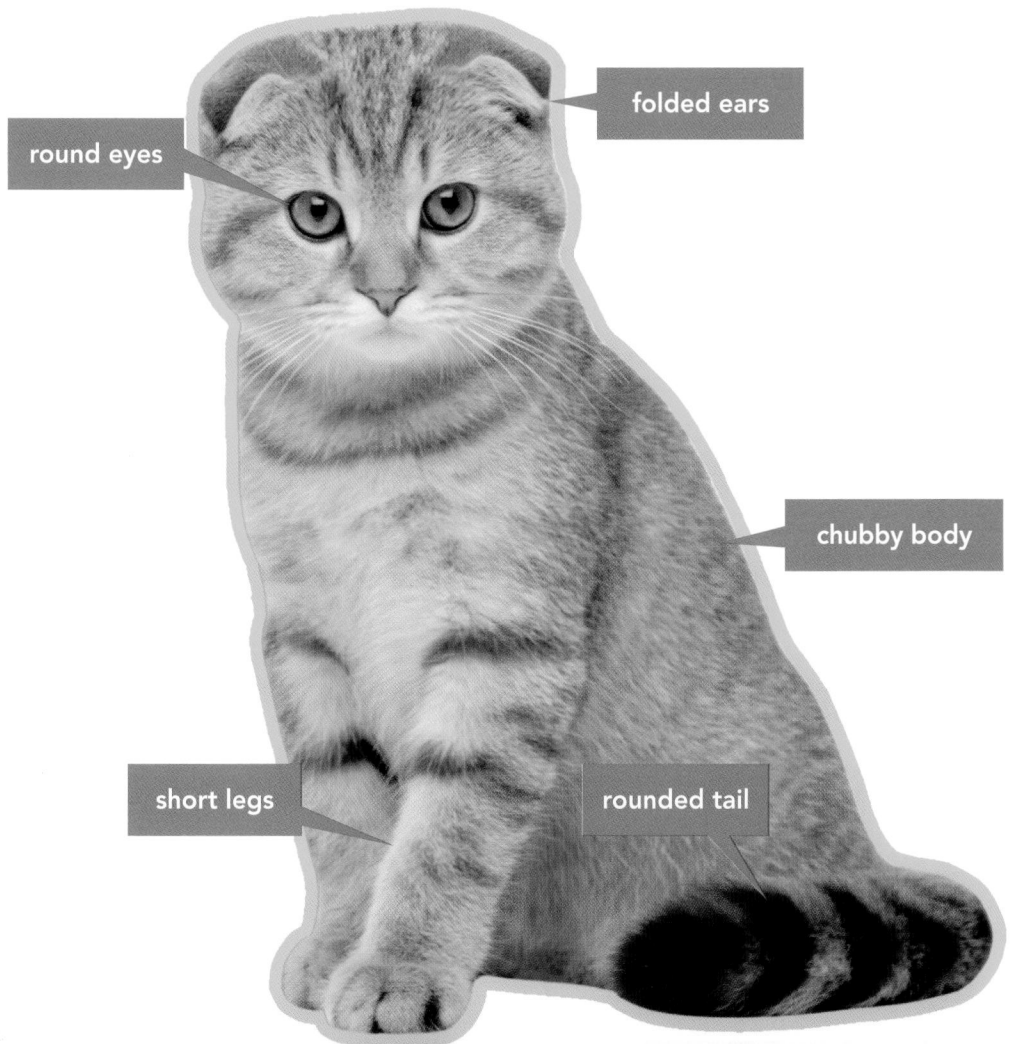

round eyes

folded ears

chubby body

short legs

rounded tail

WORDS TO KNOW

blunt – rounded, not sharp

gene – a part of DNA that is passed from parents to children and determines how a living thing will look and act

laid-back – very relaxed and calm

lop-eared – having ears that are floppy or folded

mutation – a permanent change in a living thing's genes that causes it to be different from what is normally found

plush – something that feels soft and luxurious

LEARN MORE

Books

Amstutz, Lisa. *Cats*. North Mankato, Minn.: Capstone Press, 2018.

Gagne, Tammy. *Scottish Fold Cats*. New York: AV2 by Weigl, 2018.

Leaf, Christina. *Scottish Folds*. Minneapolis: Bellwether Media, 2016.

Websites

CATS Protection: Fun Stuff for Kids
https://education.cats.org.uk/for-kids/

CFA: About the Scottish Fold
http://www.cfa.org/Breeds/BreedsSthruT/ScottishFold.aspx

Science Kids: Cats
http://www.sciencekids.co.nz/sciencefacts/animals/cat.html

INDEX

Every effort has been made to ensure that these websites are appropriate for children. However, because of the nature of the Internet, it is impossible to guarantee that these sites will remain active indefinitely or that their contents will not be altered.

Ela Area Public Library District

275 Mohawk Trail, Lake Zurich, IL 60047
(847) 438-3433
www.eapl.org

31241010299504

AUG – – 2020

D1206757